Dear Christmas: Short Christmas stories for kids

Elizabeth J. Hawks

Table of content

Dear Christmas,

I hope you are doing well and that your elves are busy creating all the amazing toys and presents for boys and girls all across the globe when you get this letter.

I have a crucial question for you today, therefore I'm writing to you. I have done well this year. I performed well in school, I helped my mom with the housework, and I was kind to my friends. I've been making a lot of effort to be a nice girl, and I was hoping you could grant me my greatest dream.

You see, my family doesn't have a lot of money for Christmas. Because of our limited resources, we sometimes have to make do without.

However, I am aware that you possess Christmas magic and have the power to do wonders.

So, dear Christmas Please bring my family a delicious, warm lunch so we may celebrate Christmas together. I assure you that we would be eternally thankful and that we would make sure to give it to others as well who are in need.

But, dear Christmas, that's not all. I still have a desire that I hope you can fulfill. Sarah, my best friend, doesn't have a very joyful home life.

She has no one to speak to and her parents are often at odds. She should experience the wonder of Christmas and understand how much I care for her.

Please bring her a special present to let her know how much she means to me and the rest of the world if it's not too much effort.

Christmas, I appreciate all you do. I have faith in you, and I have confidence that you will grant my requests.

Happy Christmas,

(Little Lizzy)

A story of fairies and Christmas

A tribe of fairies that loved nothing more than celebrating Christmas once resided in a wonderful woodland. They would get together each year to adorn the woodland with glistening lights and vibrant decorations.

The fairies gathered around a huge tree in the middle of the woodland on the eve of Christmas. As they strung decorations from the trees, they danced and sang songs. The fairies took great care to exquisitely embellish every branch.

The fairies gathered around a fire to toast marshmallows and drink hot chocolate once the tree was finished. They liked one other's company and shared tales while laughing.

The fairies gathered around the tree once again as darkness drew near. They wished for something special throughout the Christmas season while holding hands and closing their eyes. Suddenly, a lovely snowfall started to cover the woodland, giving it a more enchanting appearance.

The fairies were so happy that they danced and sang till the sun rose. The fairies prepared their gifts and left to distribute them to every animal in the forest as the dawn light peaked through the trees.

The remainder of the day was spent by the fairies bringing happiness and brightness to everyone they encountered. They were overjoyed and ecstatic because they had contributed to making this Christmas the most memorable one ever.

Once upon a time, in a faraway region, there lived a group of fairies who were responsible for ensuring that Christmas was a special time for all the good boys and girls in the world. They devoted a lot of time and effort during the whole year to utilizing their magic to produce the lovely ornaments that decorated Christmas trees, the delectable delicacies that filled stockings, and the gifts that Santa Claus would bring on Christmas Eve.

The fairies took tremendous pleasure in doing an excellent job since they liked what they did. They worked on making the most exquisite and delicate decorations for hours on end, and they made sure that every single gift was wrapped with care and finished with a dazzling ribbon.

However, the fairies started to worry as Christmas Eve drew near. They were beginning to worry since Santa Claus had still not come to collect the gifts and start his trip. What if he had had a setback? What would happen if he couldn't complete his rounds this year?

The moment the fairies were ready to give up, jolly old Saint Nick showed up at their door. He expressed gratitude to the fairies for their labor and gave them his assurance that everything would turn out OK.

Santa packed up his sleigh with all the gifts with the assistance of the fairies and started on his trip. He vanished into the night sky, bringing happiness and gladness to all the nice boys and girls, while the fairies watched.

The fairies went back to their workshop on Christmas morning as the sun rose to tidy up and get ready for the next year. They were worn out but happy since they knew they had helped make so many kids' Christmases wonderful.

The fairies so kept up their arduous efforts year after year to ensure that

Christmas was the most enchanted season of the year. And as a result of their diligence and commitment, the Christmas spirit continued to flourish, bringing pleasure and happiness to everyone.

True Friends on Christmas

Christmas is a time of pleasure and celebration, but it's also a time to pause and consider what matters most in life. A real buddy is one of the most priceless possessions we can have.

Emma and Samantha were close friends. They had been friends since they were young and had experienced everything together. They had shared dreams, secrets, and experiences, and they had always supported one another through thick and thin.

Samantha and Emma were looking forward to spending Christmas together. They intended to make cookies, decorate their houses, and exchange presents. They also anticipated spending time with their relatives and taking in all the festive occasions.

But Emma got some sad news the day before Christmas. Her distant grandma, who was in critical condition, may not survive the holiday. Emma was inconsolable. She loved her grandma dearly, and the idea of missing out on one more Christmas with her was unbearable.

Samantha didn't want her buddy to spend Christmas alone since she was aware of how much Emma was suffering. She then devised a strategy. She requested permission from Emma's parents to accompany Emma to see her grandma, and they granted it.

Samantha and Emma traveled to Emma's grandmother's residence on Christmas Eve. She was with them all day as they sang Christmas songs, read tales, and shared precious memories. Her grandmother was delighted to see her granddaughter and her close friend, and she expressed her gratitude for their visit.

The day ended with Emma's grandma passing away gently and in the company of her loved ones. While Samantha and Emma were saddened by her passing, they were also appreciative of the time they had spent with her.

Samantha and Emma left for home on Christmas Day, but their hearts were still bursting with the joy of their memorable journey. Through good times and bad, they knew they could always count on one other and that their relationship was sincere.

YET ANOTHER TALE ABOUT GENUINE BUDDIES.

Once upon a time, Holly and Ivy, two closest friends, lived in a little village tucked away in the middle of the forest. Ivy was a cheeky and lively squirrel, whereas Holly was a loving and compassionate deer.

The week before Christmas, the community was buzzing with anticipation. The air was filled with the wonderful perfume of freshly made cookies, and every home was decked up with glistening lights and holiday wreaths.

Holly and Ivy decided to visit their friend Mrs. Claus at the North Pole to assist her with the Christmas preparations because they wanted to join in on the joy.

They stumbled upon a herd of lost reindeer while they were strolling in the woodland. Although they were desperately trying to find a route back to the North Pole, the reindeer were helplessly disoriented.

Being the kind friends they were, Holly and Ivy promised to assist the wayward reindeer in returning home. They battled the blizzard together as they led the reindeer back to the North Pole.

Mrs. Claus was over the moon to meet them when they got to the North Pole. She commended Holly and Ivy for their courage and devotion and made the offer to let them assist her with the last-minute Christmas preparations.

Holly and Ivy gladly agreed, and the remainder of the week was spent decorating the sleigh, making cookies, and wrapping gifts.

Holly and Ivy gazed in awe on Christmas Eve as Santa Claus and his troop of reindeer flew into the night sky to give gifts to all the children worldwide.

Holly and Ivy realized that the true spirit of Christmas was not about getting presents, but about sharing and giving with others as they watched the sleigh depart into the distance.

They grinned and held one other warmly, certain that their genuine friendship would last forever.

Ivy and Holly had a reputation as the forest's bravest and nicest companions after that, always prepared to lend a hand to people in need.

Happy Holidays to everyone, and good night to all.

The kids and Christmas

The ground was covered with a thick layer of white snow that was falling outside slowly. The cozy glow of Christmas lights and the mouthwatering scent of cookies baking in the oven permeated the inside of the home.

The kids were gathered around the sofa watching the snow fall outside as their eyes glistened with delight. The big day was finally getting closer after what seemed like an eternity of counting down the days until Christmas.

Little Lucy said, her eyes full of amazement, "Do you think Santa will arrive tonight?"

Her elder brother Jake said, "Of course, he will!" He arrives on Christmas Eve each year to distribute gifts to all the nice boys and girls.

But what if we don't measure up? inquired Lucy, her voice edging toward fear.

They were reassured by their mother, who had just entered the room, "Don't worry, Lucy." "Santa is aware of your excellent deeds. He will undoubtedly arrive if you continue to trust in the magic of Christmas."

At their mother's comments, the kids' faces lit up, and they went back to staring out the window in anticipation of Santa.

The anticipation in the home increased as the evening went on. In addition to leaving Santa with a dish of cookies and a drink of milk, the kids placed their stockings near the fireplace. Despite their best efforts, they were unable to fall asleep due to their excitement for what the morrow would hold.

After what seemed like hours, daybreak finally came. The youngsters sprung from their beds and dashed into the living room, where they saw their stockings filled to the brim with gifts. The mass of gifts with name tags beneath the Christmas tree, though, was the highlight.

The kids tore through their gifts, shrieking with joy with every new toy or game they discovered. They couldn't help but be thankful for the enchantment of Christmas and the happiness it brought to their hearts as they played with their new possessions.

They would never forget this Christmas, and they couldn't wait for the next one to arrive so they could relive the joy.

Moral lessons for Christian kids on Christmas

There once was a kind and giving girl by the name of Lily who lived in a little community tucked away in the mountains. She was always willing to provide a hand and brighten people's days.

Lily was thrilled since it was almost Christmas. She loved every aspect of the Christmas season, including the cheerful atmosphere and the sparkling lights and ornaments. She was looking forward to seeing and exchanging presents with her friends and family.

Lily, though, noticed a difference this year. In her hamlet, some of the kids weren't as joyful as they normally were. On Christmas morning, they didn't have any new clothing to put on or presents to open. Lily's heart wrenched for them, and she was aware that she had to take action.

Lily started planning a Christmas celebration for the poorest kids in the community with the assistance of her parents. To purchase food, decorations, and presents for the kids, she solicited contributions from her friends and relatives.

Lily and her parents decorated their house like a winter wonderland the day before the celebration. The youngsters came, their eyes shining with wonder and excitement. They enjoyed excellent meals, and engaging in activities, and received presents from Lily and her family.

The only compensation Lily required was the smiles on the kids' faces. She came to see that the genuine spirit of Christmas was not about obtaining presents but about sharing love and charity with others.

Lily resolved to assist people in need over the Christmas season ever since that day. She imparted the value of giving to her friends and family and demonstrated the genuine meaning of Christmas.

So this Christmas, have Lily's example in mind and share love and happiness with others around you. We can improve the world through the good deeds we do.

Mimi and her dog 'marnie' on Christmas

Christmas preparations were underway for Mimi and her dog Marnie. On Christmas morning, Mimi was looking forward to spending time with her family and opening gifts. Marnie was looking forward to the delectable delicacies and more attention she would get.

Marnie and Mimi's day was spent making cookies, trimming the tree, and wrapping presents. Taste-testing the cookies and barking at the decorations to make sure they were hung correctly were also ways Marnie contributed.

Mimi and Marnie cuddled up by the fireside on Christmas Eve to read a holiday tale. Marnie listened carefully while wiggling her tail and perking up her ears.

Mimi and Marnie were the first ones up on Christmas morning. To see what Santa had left for them, they rushed downstairs. Marnie was overjoyed to see a new chew toy and a bag of dog biscuits, while Mimi was ecstatic to discover a new doll and a sparkling outfit beneath the tree.

Marnie and Mimi enjoyed each other's company and played with their new toys all day. They made a snowman, engaged in a snowball war, then went on a stroll in the snow.

Mimi and Marnie once again huddled by the hearth as the day drew to an end. Marnie's tail wagged in gratitude as Mimi congratulated her for being the finest friend she could ever hope for.

Marnie and Mimi had the happiest Christmas ever, which was filled with love, laughing, and pleasure.

Dear kids,

Without Jesus, Christmas tales are incomplete.

Christmas is a time for pleasure and celebration, but it's also a moment to reflect on the holiday's actual significance. All kids should study the Christmas narrative, which is centered on the life of Jesus Christ.

When King Herod governed the country of Israel, Jesus was born in a barn near Bethlehem. Mary, a young lady who had been selected by God to be the mother of the Son of God, gave birth to him.

A group of shepherds were taking care of their sheep in the pastures close by when Jesus was born. The shepherds hurried to the stable to meet the infant King after an angel informed them of the birth of the baby Jesus.

As Jesus matured, his compassion and intellect astounded everyone. He assisted those in need and shared the love of God with others. He also performed miracles, such as curing the ill and reviving the dead.

In the end, one of Jesus' disciples betrayed him, and the Romans had to take him into custody. He was tried, given the death penalty, and crucified.

But Jesus was free from the grip of even death. Jesus appeared to many people after rising from the grave on the third day after his death, demonstrating that he was in fact the Son of God.

Jesus' life is a tale of love, giving, and redemption. It is a tale that teaches us the value of kindness and compassion toward others as well as the strength of forgiveness.

Let's keep in mind the teachings of Jesus' life narrative this Christmas. In order to love and care for people around us, promote joy and pleasure across the globe, and become more like him, let us endeavor to do these things.

The End

www.ingramcontent.com/pod-product-compliance
Lightning Source LLC
LaVergne TN
LVHW020532160826
845677LV00015B/4022
9798369788912